A Million Less Prisoners Please

A
Million
Less
Prisoners
Please

Reverend Mike Wanner

Copyright
Rev. Mike Wanner
September 12, 2018

Selected Images Used by License

"Prison Presents" Tab
"Healing Presents" Tab

http://www.AngelRaphaelSpeaks.com

Introduction

I had written 61 books about prisons that had gone before this one that observed patterns and the influences which could help set up for a societal reassessment of standard prison procedures. Reframing and reprioritization could help revamp the prison experience for a lot of people and mitigate collateral damage.

It seems that the powers for management to use are very rigid. The voters could empower administrative changes if and when updated legislation is put to the vote, but proposals are limited in the area of rehabilitation and Re-Entry readiness education.

Unfortunately, the changes that are being considered may be less than optimal for the future benefit of the broader society including prison staff and taxpayers.

We need to step up and deal with realities in a fundamental objective and balanced way that can optimize multitudes of lives for the present and future occupants of our world.

I would like to start with a list of priorities for consideration:

1. Invite law enforcement and spiritual leaders to sit down and set some safety guidelines to minimize conflicts between the authorities and free citizens. A source concept guide to consider is - "*Compliance with Dignity.*"

2. Invite taxpayers to reassess our values.

3. Invite the nation to start writing about positive actions that the citizens can Initiate to reboot our prison guidelines.

4. Develop a broad-based plan for gaining ground in the battle for a revitalized America.

5. Add safety to our communities.

6. Develop modest treatment criteria for willing prisoners to take charge of any addictions.

7. Develop modest treatment criteria for willing prisoners to take charge of their thinking.

8. Provide a path to rehabilitation for those who self-select it.

9. Optimize some opportunities without cost to those who are self-starters and self-motivated.

10. Create coaching opportunities for prisoners to support and coach each other.

11. Develop an opportunity for prisoners to become school teacher's consultants to help teachers understand the issues of inner-city children.

Table of Contents

Copyright 2
Introduction 3
Table of Contents 5
Dedication 6
1 - Why I am Writing This Book 7
2 - Disclaimer 9
3 - Building New Beneficial Paradigms 11
4 - Media Can Lead the Way 12
5 - Titles for Movies I would like To Watch 13
6 - Ground Rules For This Goal Request 14
7 - The Very Beginning 15
8 - Encountering the Authorities 18
9 - Post Arrest Processing Trauma 19
10 - Addiction Cost Shifting 20
11 - Sentencing 21
12 - Daily Prison Operations Enhancement 23
13 - Presents for Prisoners, Their Families 25
14 - "Prison Rehabilitation" 27
15 - Improving the Lives of Prisoners 29
16 - The Other Book Titles 31
17 - Wrap Up 33
18 - Thank You 34
19 - Don't Worry Ever 35
20 - Books Category Resources 36
21 - Angels Please Prayers 37
22 - Private Channeling 38
23 - Reverend Mike Wanner 39

Dedication

This book is

Dedicated

To setting

Rehabilitation

as

The Primary Goal

for

Prisons!

1 - Why I am Writing This Book

The responsibilities of Leadership of all kinds can be hard work. The legislative process that empowers the administrative oversight of prisons is rigid so interpretation can be challenging.

While a lot of stories may be written about the need for changes, I have not been aware of an abundance of How To books in the Prison Leadership niche. Delighted was I to see that in the sixth position was a book I wrote.

Candidly, huge problems may be the avoidance of being the messenger when the topic is strongly condemned with little contrast that could inspire anybody.

My books resist the reactive complaining inclination and strive to focus on the potential for creative thought to showcase things differently and frugally to generate ways to reframe possibilities in order to get some initial traction.

The legal system is precise, and that is necessary for them to comply with the rulings of the court. There is not the potential for clarification that can exist in many private businesses.

Restructuring to allow legal and proper prisoner enterprises that could be taken away with them when prisoners exit could be a key to meaningful Re-entry for prisoners and their families.

The challenges for prisons, prison staff, prisoners and all connected persons are enormous. We need new ideas for better results.

Invitations to discussions could allow an opportunity for the community to understand that all ideas will be examined and evaluated but a component of all proposals needs to be frugality. The goals should consistently embrace cost savings by wise choices that avoid new budget hurdles.

Teaming with others can remedy any old feelings of being ignored and isolated. Being active in masterminding a fresh start can be supportive of each participants optimization of their days. Choice discernment can spread the impact.

The administration can help people know the best way to cooperate. Knowing the rules to open a door of opportunity can be helpful.

Many of the societal problems that we have today have emotional roots in the avoidance of taking responsibility for one's actions. The prisoners can learn responsibility they can share with the broader community.

Information exceeds ignorance when seeking personal peace.

2 - Disclaimer

I, the author, am not involved with a particular prison or system or prisoner as many readers maybe, but I have talked to many prisoners during Hospital Pastoral Visitations.

I am sharing what is coming to me in an effort to spread understanding and trigger conversations that can be helpful. It may be that the discussion needs finessing and I invite your wisdom into the mix.

My guidance has suggested that a lot can be done. I have detailed my views which are not the expert positions of one of your leaders or another expert who might be helpful here. I have written a lot about healing in general and in prisons, and the Healing Books list and the Prison Books list is at the website http://www.AngelRaphaelSpeaks.com

That website also has pages titled "Prison Presents" and "Healing Presents" which offer the books that are free on Kindle and the dates they are Free.

This book identifies the real goal of all my books about incarceration. My goal is fewer prisoners behind the walls and more who exit with the skills to never come back.

The complexity of all the issues that prisoners and prison staff have to deal with can lead to a very stressful environment, and that complicates the processes and raises the stress for everybody.

Stress has been so much in my awareness for so long that I actually have a whole separate website which deals with it, and the URL is http://StressReleaseCoach.com.

Please be aware that nowhere in my books is any recommendation of releasing prisoners who are not ready. There is a lot however about helping prisoners to find information so that they can repurpose their lives for the betterment of the community.

Note

I have also written about Dialogues, and I invite you to consider sharing your ideas in public and with me in the optimal format specified below. The core message about the series can be found for free at http://angelraphaelspeaks.com/prison-possible/ I invite your consideration of this tool to further dialogue and promote progress in all the areas of your interest.

The desired format for Dialogues is a single Page Configuration >150 words <220 Words, in a 6 x9 book format with all .5 margins, Title Font 20 Pt. Times New Roman, Body Font 14 Pt. Times New Roman. Adherence to the desired template will go a long way to simplify the process for me. Thank You.

3 - Building New Beneficial Paradigms

Media is quite good at sensory stimulation and maybe overdoing entertainment to a level that is no longer beneficial. There is a catastrophizing of circumstances that can leave people feeling helpless and hopeless that can hyperstimulate those who are vulnerable.

Powerless people can be distressed and evolve into a depression of personal vitality. We see in America that the norm has shifted too much in one direction and there needs to be a call to the middle ground.

While it is hard to challenge successful businesses that create jobs and provide entertainment, it is essential that the balance of awareness for the citizens be reasonable.

Too many businesses that compete can kill the profits for all and kill the golden goose. If a person eats the same dish every night for a long time, it will become tiresome and be avoided eventually.

The spectrum of options needs diversity to provide a continuation and consistency for the benefit of users. Let's encourage the variety that spices up lives and leads to broad-based abundance in all areas.

Creative people abound, and it may be an optimal time for successful media businesses to create trial balloons for future entertainment impacts. Empowerment may be crucial to success.

4 - Media Can Lead the Way

Media knows what sells so none of us can expect that the Hollywood standards can be revamped because a minister wrote a book. The nation is full, of many families, and one of the biggest challenges for them is to find entertainment that each of them can enjoy together. Serving new families can help profits.

Media is aware of the needs and is bringing unusual ideas forward in strategic ways that are sharing situations that encourage understanding and shift perceptions. Congratulations on doing that.

To move further forward, let's brainstorm. We need a national talk about police and citizens interactions.

Movie and TV producers could find a goldmine in digging into the content that I wrote about in my book Compliance With Dignity. Citizens of all kinds need to know about the severity of conflicts between police and those they stop.

My book encourages simple ways to consider expectation for the Ministers and the Police to team up and create practical rules of Interaction that could save lives. My ideas are only the seed of a potential change that could look differently at the end of a developed plan.

Media and other Content creators can surely come up with better ideas than I and I encourage you all to do so.

5 - Titles for Movies I would like To Watch

Teach the Children They Are Loved

Toy Guns and Real Ones Are Dangerous

Schools Can Help Prevent Incarceration

Prisoners Can Reality Check Ideas

Segmented So Prisoners Can Find Quiet

Segment So Prisoners Can Think

Segment So Prisoners Can Learn

24 Hour Prison Space Usage is Ideal

Prisoner Safety Can Save Money

Taxpayers Can Have a Prison Cost Break

6 - Ground Rules For This Goal Request

I hate to be the adult in the room, but participants should be aware of what kind of things are welcome in this goal request and what to avoid. Respondents are requested to be mindful of the following suggestions so their efforts will be well received and more likely to be embraced. My ideas are below but all facilities, of course, can write their own rules.

We Consider Respectful Suggestions Only

Financial Goal Is No Additional Expense

Space Goal Is More Space Per Prisoner

We Invite Mental Health suggestions

We Invite Addictions Program Suggestions

We Invite Gang Possibilities Suggestions

We Invite Depression Program Suggestions

We Invite Safety Enhancement Suggestions

7 - The Very Beginning

"A Very Good Place To Start"
{Sound Of Music - Do-Re-Mi Lyrics}

Schools are where the learning of children starts. The interactions there can be helpful or hurtful.

The best teachers can be overloaded with students and unable to humanely customize their programs to accommodate the needs of all class members. The size of school budgets can be impressive, but the needs of students in different communities can vary greatly.

So, what is adequate in many districts may be insufficient in adjacent cities. The school administrators have their plates full in trying to keep everything going.

It's highly likely that you can find many stories throughout the year in your local media about the education costs where you live. There are about 6,000 prisons in America, and that can cover a whole lot of school districts.

If you can remember your school experiences, you might recall that children who were different could be isolated and bullied. I have read that the frequently estimated population of the prison system has been about 2.3 million and those citizens can have approximately 2.7 million children.

Schools could be hard places for children of prisoners to learn.

If one is not accepted at their school, social life can be minimal. The struggles of these children can go a long way toward aggravating the parents at home and in prison.

The public school systems still have the responsibility for the education of all students. Misery can go around the schools and the prisons rapidly and further complicate the efforts of all staff members.

In line-and-staff organizations like schools and prisons and businesses and armies, there is a need to follow the protocol and procedures for staff members to stay employed there. Guidelines are not always clear enough for non-executives to understand and apply.

Amongst the books that I have written are some ideas that may help and my 61st book about prison talks about *Prison Segmentation for Inner City Teacher Advisors*.
Listening is one of the most powerful skills that managers can use to cross thought boundaries which defend against change.

Please take a minute and conceptualize how things could change if cooperating teams could be heard and their ideas digested, sorted and prioritized. Imagine also the following:

> 1. Teachers are learning enough about the inner cities to be savvy enough to ask prisoners advisors the meaning of what the kids are saying.

2. Students being able to be understood by the academics oriented teachers that have been hired to teach them.

3. Prisoner advisors who have a positive focus for their days that can help children and maybe even their own.

4. Students' needs being heard easier as their teachers struggle less to comprehend what they say.

8 - Encountering the Authorities

There is a lot of sentiment in the United States about entitlement, and I do not wish to comment on any of that because the arguments all make some rational sense.

I wrote a little book about Compliance because so much is communicated with the eyes of fear that can trigger rejection of all parties by the other and set the stage for explosive conflict.

I respectfully ask all who read this to invite a series of conversations between law enforcement representatives and representatives of interested groups and ministries.

I would really love to see that Happen in the Cradle of Liberty – Philadelphia for illustrative purposes. Liberty is a treasure.

It is essential that guidelines be developed because symbols of compliance and respect can be pivotal to the safety of everybody.

The People at Risk include:
    Citizens
    Officers of the Law
    Bystanders
    Children of Citizens
    Children of Officers of the Laws
    Children Who see it on television.
    Adults who see it on television

9 - Post Arrest Processing Trauma

There is a lot of post-arrest processing trauma that is seen clearly on the television sets throughout the nation. The issues depicted can show conspiracies against those arrested very graphically which can be a depressing and fearful depiction like a horror movie which may even traumatize some folks.

There seems to be both a statutory and futile defensive sentiment in the United States about defense with less than optimal substance. I wrote another book about using prisoners as advocates for supporting those who are arrested who might be able to offer a bit of perspective and solace to the pre-trial stressed out candidates for prison.

A big part of that book was about trying to allow those helping to do a courtesy call to the booked person's employer to decrease the likelihood of losing their jobs and careers and livelihoods because of an arrest.

Employers who get no notification could be harmed because an employee did not show up as planned. If that employer is hurt financially, they may have cause for termination which could damage the standing of the detainee and their ability to support their family.

This is also important to the local government which does not need more people out of work to support.

10 - Addiction Cost Shifting

Another Reason to communicate with employers is that their relationship with employees who are addicts could put them into treatment that the community could need not pay for. Quick actions would be needed,To avoid the addiction expense of treatment, and the post-arrest pre-trial processing system could prove a lifesaver to both the citizen and the community coffers.

There seems to be a void in the hearts of many people, and they crave something to fill that need. God and the Angels would be great, but addicts usually choose something stronger.

I am hopeful that You and I and others can offer some wisdom that can help a lot of people to make healthy choices in that regard.

I would encourage all to teach, write and speak about common sense approaches to the addiction issues that confront our prison community to align with rehabilitation efforts.

On the Angel Please Prayers page later in this book will be pictured my effort to help. The Web Link below the book cover shown will take you to a page in that website that has the Core Messages from the book on drop-down pages.

Everyone does not believe in Angels, so more options are needed. Can you write a message that can help?

11 - Sentencing

The system of Jurisprudence is very complicated, and that intricate system makes progress difficult even when agencies are trying hard. The detailed system dynamics need to be unraveled, and that can be time-consuming and stressful to the whole system.

I am not proposing but suggesting that one idea to consider is merely changing the universe of prison rules by going back to the source legislation and create an authority that can supersede existing criteria.

I wrote a book called the *Answer to Sentencing: Help Judges Cut Minimums* that offers a discussion about a survey of judges where about fifty percent of them indicated that the mandatory minimums should be malleable at the discretion of the presiding judge. I also was aware that the 50% of the judges were roughly in alignment with an Angel Raphael message I channeled that we could cut prison costs by 47%.

My original interest was triggered by a story in the press of a Federal Judge in Nashville who quit the bench because of a job requirement that he follow the mandatory rules.

My opinion is that the Judges are in the best position to know the details of each case and should have the power to choose. The voting booth is the supreme authority in this country, and all voters could vote for the highest good. I include below a form from that book that citizens could send their representatives and declare their support for Judicial discretion.

Proposed Declaration to ---------------
{Modified slightly from Chapter 16 of *Answer to Sentencing: Help Judges Cut Minimums*}

"We the people of _____ wish to convey to you, our esteemed representatives, that we are tremendously unhappy with the volume of our brother and sister citizens who are currently incarcerated. We feel that the laws in place are antiquated and threaten our freedom.

With all due respect, we implore you as our representatives to take on the task of fixing this problem. The social fabric of our communities needs to be protected from burdensome legal complications of the lengthy sentences created by the Mandatory Minimums.

We assert herewith the will of the people to empower the Judges to cut the sentences for non-violent offenders at the discretion of the Judges when they deem appropriate.

We would like to see the sentencing cut substantially and declare that 47% (Forty-Seven Percent) is not an unrealistic number. We would actually prefer if the average cut exceeded 22% (Twenty-Two Percent).

We trust Your diligence in the compliance with our wishes."

12 - Daily Prison Operations Enhancement

A large portion of my writing has been about programs to consider, and another group is about space use, and I call that segmentation. Optimal space use could increase the spatial perceptions that can soothe individuals and provide more quiet time and less distraction.

Now everybody is in bed at the same time, and Everybody is circulating at the same times. Changing to three shifts could decrease the numbers of prisoner flowing at any given time by up to a third and reduce the likelihood of conflicts.

1. Prison Segmentation for Safety, Sanity, Security, Peace & Space
2. Prison Segmentation for Security
3. Prison Segmentation for Mental Peace
4. Prison Segmentation for Joint Ventures
5. Prison Segmentation for Startup Ideas
6. Prison Segmentation for Your Rehabilitation: R U Ready?
7. Prison Segmentation for Family Villages
8. Prison Segmentation for Senior Prisoners
9. Prison Segmentation for Coaching Clubs
10. Prison Segmentation for Miracles
11. Prison Segmentation for A Prison Game Show
12. Prison Segmentation for Spousal Support
13. Prison Segmentation for Exit Contracts
14. Prison Segmentation for Sentence Segments
15. Prison Segmentation for Overnight Visitors
16. Prison Segmentation for Lifer Purpose Plan
17. Prison Segmentation for Prisoner Guards Share Freedoms
18. Prison Segmentation for Defense Support
19. Prison Segmentation for Waiver Design
20. Prison Segmentation for A Job Fair
21. Prison Segmentation for Sound Healing Drug Alternative
22. Prison Segmentation for Pre-Trial Laptop Workers
23. Prison Segmentation for Spiral Path Circuit Connections
24. Prison Segmentation for Video Notes
25. Prison Segmentation for Premium Prison
26. Prison Segmentation for Inner City Teacher Advisors.

The segments have precise target projects, and they fit in with all the other books about prison possibilities. The books rotate free on Kindle - http://angelraphaelspeaks.com/christmas/.

13 - Presents for Prisoners, Their Families and the public Started Christmas Day 2017

I am a Circle of Miracles Inter-Faith Minister and live in Philadelphia, and I channel the Angel of Healing – Archangel Raphael who has motivated me to write a lot about healing. It started as little e-books that I published separately in small sets that I gave away and eventually had me channel about three hundred messages is a series called Angel Raphael Speaks.

There are only 14 messages about prisons in the original book out of the approximately one hundred there. Eight came later in Volume 2 and 3 Those 22 messages spurred an invitation that took me to write the 60+ prison books that I have now published about prisons and saving the American economy from death by prison costs.

The 60+ books about prison possibilities alone and the current list are available at http://angelraphaelspeaks.com/prison-books.

Most of the books are available FREE one at a time on a rotating basis as presents every five days or so through Kindle to all who would like them. The release schedule is routinely updated and available at
http://angelraphaelspeaks.com/christmas/

The schedule can also be accessed at the *Prison Presents* Tab at http://www.AngelRaphaelSpeaks.com

Angel Raphael Speaks – Prisons was a spinoff e-book of the Angel Raphael Speaks Channelings. It is available as a separate e-book on Kindle and is also included in the book *Angel Raphael Speaks Volume One.*

The whole set of 22 prisons messages was released separately as *Penitentiary Edition of Angel Raphael Speaks.*

I have no expertise in prisons but listen well to Spirit. I have given away thousands of my healing books to veterans and others.

I am also an ordained Metaphysical Minister through the International Metaphysical Ministry in Sedona, AZ.

May all who read this be blessed AND SO IT IS!

May all who download these books begin to see new possibilities for prisoners to reboot their lives and find a place where they can contribute to society once again. The costs of incarceration are out of control, and they drain the government coffers and keep funding from schools and other beneficial programs.

We all need to regroup and offer kindness and opportunities for the financial safety of our nation and the security of our neighborhoods. We Are all in it together.

14 - "Prison Rehabilitation"
{A Message from Set 10 of the Angel Raphael Speaks Series}
{A Channeled Message from Angel Raphael}

"The answer to prison rehabilitation is **Purpose**" (A purpose for each prisoner's life.) While some institutions may have initiated programs to engage their residents, the feeling of a purposeful life brings a new reality to the incarcerated.

Purposes to consider will be ones that work for the incarcerated as well as the society which actually pays the bills. Special characteristics to include would be the creation of a feeling of accomplishment generated by prisoner effort and drastic cost savings for the institution.

The real loss to prisons is wasted time, no productivity and no graciousness of interactive genius. If invited, the right use of time can provide different results than now seen.

There is no profit to society when cruelness is applied to the control of citizens. There may be temporary security, but that comes at a big price to the potential of all.

The best way to learn about what is possible is to listen to the troubled stories of the incarcerated people. Their genius can be tapped by mining information about how to fill the gap that they slipped into so that newer walkers on their path can find the gap filled by their charity of sharing their pain as a love patch to the sinkholes of society.

The answers through this channel are coming differently than most could conceive and that is because neither you nor I have a job whose agenda has its own needs.

You ask to imagine how much can be cut from prison costs to maintain security, improve lives, create new industry and improve the focus, flavor, and flair of American life and you dowsed for an answer. You got 47% reduction, and you questioned your dowsing. Your questioning is wise because there is a huge industry that has roots in the status quo.

While that is true, your answer has potential that will serve the ones that would resist the initiatives that flow from the message. Their positions are survivable as is for a time unknown but their openness to change can also serve their security.

The change will happen even if they choose to use their money to resist the inevitable avalanche of change. Their opportunities are paramount in the areas of personal safety for all and the possibility to create new meaningful arrangements that are self-sustaining for all levels of the resident base and those employed in the industry."   ARS 10

15 - Improving the Lives of Prisoners

Preparing for Re-Entry

Teach A Prisoner to Fish (Survive)

A quotation potentially derived from a Chinese saying that is also possibly sourced from a Mrs. Drumond book in 1885 is often declared as:

"G<u>ive</u> <u>a</u> <u>man</u> <u>a</u> <u>fish</u>, <u>and</u> <u>you</u> <u>feed</u> <u>him</u> <u>for</u> <u>a</u> <u>day</u>; <u>teach</u> <u>a</u> <u>man</u> <u>to</u> <u>fish</u>, <u>and</u> <u>you</u> <u>feed</u> <u>him</u> <u>for</u> <u>a</u> <u>lifetime</u> "

Can we as a community be selective enough to monitor participation and interests enough so that incremental baby steps of self-reliance are noticed, acknowledged, celebrated and built upon?

When I was young, a long time ago, a lot of cities had spiritual "Reading Rooms." People may not have read as often back then as some providers may have wished but they may have found some peace there. I think it is fair to say that lower-income citizens may look at books even less now. A video is an option.

Perhaps prisons might consider an updated adaptation that could function as a series of available viewing stations where moderately uplifting messages could be viewed by request from a list of possible choices.

Prison viewing centers could be safety zones for learning facilitated on a regular basis by the incarcerated who chose to participate and learn as they hold a representation of peace from the hectic world outside their doors. As the awareness of possibilities builds information seekers can turn the spirals of their lives higher.

As success opportunities abound, the participation can grow, and patterns of involvement can bloom and seed further possibilities for future residents.

The old ways do not work well anymore. The pushing against the old ways also does not seem to work well because the people responsible for the old rules have been pushing up daisies for a long time.

We as a nation need a simple, fresh start for the incarcerated going forward. We can remember backward as we attain a more current point of reasonable treatment methods that promote rehabilitation that works and is cost effective.

There is no suggestion here that favoritism be applied just the inclusion of options that can dramatically enhance the efficiency of our facilities and the reduction of unnecessary consequential damage to the families of all residents.

16 - The Other Book Titles

Beside the Segmentation books listed above, there were thirty-five others titles which included the following:

Angel Raphael Speaks Volume 4: Angels, Addicts, Alcoholics & Prisoners - Oh Yeah!
Angel Raphael Speaks Volume 5: Prisoners Caring for Alcoholics - Australia In Miniature   Projects Intro
Angel Raphael Speaks Volume 6: Prisoners Caring for Addicts Australia In Miniature For Addicts
Prison Jobs Now: Providing Care For Addicts And Alcoholics
Angel Raphael Speaks - Prisons (A Kindle only book -2013)
Contained Care Communities: Concept
Australia In Miniature
Prison Possibilities Dialogue Series: Concept
Prison Possibilities Dialogue Series: Volume 2 Dialogues
Prison Possibilities Dialogue Series: Volume 3 Dialogues
Prison Possibilities Dialogue Series: Volume 4 Dialogues
Prison Possibilities Dialogue Series: Volume 5 Dialogues
Prison Possibilities Voluntary Exile: Concept
Prison Possibilities Correction Coaches: Concept
Prison Possibilities for Mexicans: Is A Boat Better than A Wall?
Prison Possibilities Family Time: A Reason to Thrive!
Prison Genius Pool: "So Much Genius In Jail."
Prison Possibilities Access Systems: Prisoner Access by Request
Prisoner's Lawyers Can Save The American Economy: Make A Buck Doing It & Be Thanked!

Prisoner Family Talks, Days, Stays & Vacations: Connecting Helps Healing

Prisoner Writing Projects: Write To Heal, Start Over & Reconnect

Prison Cell Clearing & Blessing: Clear Entities, Chase Ghosts, and & Create Sacred Space

Prisoner Professors: Show You Are Aware Create Change With Care

Prison Reiki? Maybe Someday? A Gateway To Help Heal Prisons & America?

Judges and An Angel Rule On Possibilities: We Can Cut Sentences & Prison Costs

Ideas For Prison Wardens: Leadership Is Not Easy

Solitary Community: Could Community Support Cut Costs and Issues?

Prisoner Projects Communication Teams: Communications Can Change Lives

Motivating & Empowering Prisoners?

Dowsing for Prisoners; Answers from Above

Ex-Prisoner Possibilities With Real Estate Investors

Prison Prayer Book

Answer To Sentencing

The 60th Book on Prison Hope

The books rotate free on Kindle

"Prison Presents" Tab

http://www.AngelRaphaelSpeaks.com

17 - Wrap Up

There are many ways to approach the goal of A Million fewer Prisoners and success will be determined by the ability of readers to encourage possibilities where they wish to see them.

If you need motivation, just project the number of prisoners in your state or jurisdiction and multiply the amount by $39,000 to get a low estimate of the yearly costs to you and other taxpayers.

Next just imagine that each prison managed to pick an idea that will work to help minimize occupancy just a little bit and cut costs while making zero safety and security compromises. If you like the total saving, you can ask your representatives to repeat every year going forward.

The jurisdictions are mutually exclusive, and each can get on board any of the ideas and initiate change or determine the concepts and suggestions are not possible there.

Every citizen who has the power to vote can help improve the incarceration problem. When you talk to politicians, please consider informing them politely if you want to rehabilitate prisoners and cut costs.

18 - Thank You

For
Considering
These
Ideas

19 - Don't Worry Ever

It Does Not Help Prayer Still Does!

Resource: http://Create-A-Prayer.com

20 - Books Category Resources at www.Amazon.com

Distant Healing (or Mail List) e-mail mikewann@voicenet.com

Veterans Healing Six Pack plus 2
http://angelraphaelspeaks.com/healing-books/veterans/

PTSD Power Pack
http://angelraphaelspeaks.com/healing-books/ptsd/

Angel Raphael Speaks Series & Other Angel Books
http://angelraphaelspeaks.com/

Reiki
http://angelraphaelspeaks.com/healing-books/reiki/

Children
http://angelraphaelspeaks.com/healing-books/children/

Emergency Medical Kindness
http://angelraphaelspeaks.com/healing-books/emergency-medical-kindness/

Cancer
http://angelraphaelspeaks.com/healing-books/cancer/

Addictions
http://angelraphaelspeaks.com/healing-books/addictions/

Miscellaneous Healing
http://angelraphaelspeaks.com/healing-books/misc-healing/

Prison Books - 50+ Prison Books
http://angelraphaelspeaks.com/prison-books/

21 - Angels Please Prayers

Addict's
Angels of Healing Selected
Help Me to Stay Directed
Come To Me From The Sky
I Am Ready to Succeed Not Try
If I Don't Invite You In
I Might Not Win
I Have Been Lost For Too Long
Help Me To Stay Strong

Alcoholic's
Angels of Healing On High
Help Me to Stay Dry
Come To Me From The Sky
I Am Ready to Succeed Not Try
If I Don't Invite You In
I Might Not Win
I Have Been Lost For Too Long
Help Me To Stay Strong

From

http://AngelRaphaelSpeaks.com/AAAAAAA/
The Link Above Has the Core Messages from the book on drop-down pages.

22 - Private Channeling

Angel Raphael Speaks a series of free messages that are channeled through Reverend Mike Wanner for the Highest good and Highest Healing of all concerned.

Many questions arise about Reverend Mike doing private channeling, and he does help with that so E-mail him.

Reverend Mike is available worldwide as a psychic channel, emotional release facilitator, spiritual energy practitioner & teacher, and public speaker. He looks forward to meeting you soon! Email - mikewann@voicenet.com 215-342-1270

PRIVATE SPIRITUAL READINGS/channelings or Spiritual Healing Sessions: Telephone or in person.

Rev. Mike is available for individual, intuitive one-on-one sessions with you, his Guide Family, and your Guides. He helps by offering clarity on emotional situations about your life, your purpose, your spirituality, and your release of stuffed emotions and cellular memory.

Connect to the love of your Guides today!

For more information, Please visit

http://angelraphaelspeaks.com/channel/

23 - Reverend Mike Wanner

Rev. Mike Wanner started his spiritual and ministerial studies with Reiki in 1993 and had studied seven styles of Reiki in the U.S., Japan, Canada, Denmark, and Australia. He is certified to teach. He became certified to teach Integrated Energy Therapy in 1999 and co-taught the first IET class of the new Millennium. Mike began dowsing in 2001.

Ordained as an Interfaith Minister of the Circle of Miracles Ministry and a Metaphysical Minister of the International Metaphysical Ministry, Rev. Mike practices and teaches spiritual energy therapies in the Philadelphia Area.

Rev. Mike holds ministerial degrees from the University of Metaphysics and the University of Sedona. He is a Pastoral Care Associate at Jefferson - Frankford Hospital. He taught at the National Academy of Massage Therapy and Health Sciences.

Rev. Mike was a faculty member of the Medical Mission Sister's Center for Human Integration's School of Integrated Body/Mind Therapies in Fox Chase, Philadelphia, PA for twelve years.

For a complete Biography, Please visit

http://ReverendMikeWanner.com/Bio